The Crystal Path

Healing Energies and Meditative Journeys

Amanda M Clarke

Daily Guidance
SERIES

Koru Lifestylist

KORU (Maori:NZ)
A symbol of spiritual growth and spiritual connection.

Crystals of the Chakras

Crown Chakra	Clear Quartz
Third Eye Chakra	Lapis Lazuli
Throat Chakra	Amazonite
Heart Chakra	Rose Quartz
Solar Plexus Chakra	Pyrite
Sacral Chakra	Carnelian
Root Chakra	Red Jasper

Copyright © 2024 by Koru Lifestylist

All rights reserved. All content, materials, and intellectual property in this book or any other platform owned by Koru Lifestylist are protected by copyright laws. This includes text, images, graphics, videos, audio, software, and any other form of content that may be produced by Koru Lifestylist.

No part of this content may be reproduced, distributed, or transmitted in any form or by any means without the prior written permission of Koru Lifestylist. This means that you cannot copy, reproduce, or use any of the content in this book for commercial or personal purposes without the express written consent of Koru Lifestylist.

Unauthorized use of any copyrighted material owned by Koru Lifestylist may result in legal action being taken against you. Koru Lifestylist reserves the right to pursue all available legal remedies against any individual or entity found to be infringing on its copyright.

In summary, Koru Lifestylist © 2024 holds exclusive rights to all the content produced by it, and any unauthorized use of such content will result in legal action.

How to Use This Book

Welcome to your journey with crystal healing and daily guidance. This book is designed to help you connect with the healing energies of crystals and provide you with daily insights and guidance. Here's how to make the most of your experience:

Step 1: Clear the Energies of the Book
Before you begin, it's important to cleanse the book to ensure it is free from any lingering energies. This can be done in several ways:

Smudging: Light a sage stick or palo santo and gently waft the smoke over the book.

Crystal Cleansing: Place a cleansing crystal, such as Selenite or Clear Quartz, on top of the book for a few minutes.

Sound: Use a singing bowl, bell, or chime to create a sound vibration around the book.

Step 2: Invoke the Spirits or Angels
To invite higher energies and guidance into your reading, you may want to perform an incantation. Hold the book in your hands, close your eyes, and say:

"Spirits and angels, guides of light,
I call upon you on this night.
Bless this book with love and grace,
Help me find my sacred space.
Guide my heart and clear my mind,
With crystal wisdom intertwined.
So mote it be."

Feel free to modify the incantation to align with your beliefs and intentions.

Step 3: Set Your Intention or Ask a Question
Before you begin flipping through the pages, take a moment to set your intention or ask a specific question. This helps to focus your energy and aligns the book's guidance with your needs. You might say:

My intention for today is to find peace and clarity."
or
"What do I need to know to move forward with confidence?"

Step 4: Choose Your Method
Decide how you will navigate through the book. You can:

Flip through the pages: Slowly flip through the book, either forward or backward, until you feel an intuitive nudge to stop.

Use a wand, bookmark, or feather: Close your eyes and run the chosen object along the edges of the pages. When you feel guided, stop and open the book.

Open randomly: Simply open the book at any random point, trusting that the right page will reveal itself.

Step 5: Read and Reflect
Once you've landed on a page, read the healing interpretation of the crystal and the accompanying meditation. Take your time to absorb the message and reflect on how it applies to your current situation.

Step 6: Meditate with the Crystal
Follow the short meditation provided on the page to connect with the crystal's energy. Hold a physical crystal if you have one, or simply visualize the crystal's energy enveloping you. Allow yourself to be fully present in the meditation, embracing the healing and guidance it offers.

Step 7: Journal Your Experience
After your meditation, take a few moments to journal your thoughts, feelings, and any insights you gained. This helps to deepen your understanding and track your progress over time. You will find journaling pages at the back of this book.

Tips for Daily Practice

Consistency: Make this practice a part of your daily routine, whether in the morning to set the tone for your day or in the evening to reflect and unwind.

Openness: Approach each session with an open heart and mind, ready to receive whatever message the crystals have for you.

Gratitude: End each session with a moment of gratitude for the guidance and healing you've received.

This book is a powerful tool for personal growth and spiritual connection. By integrating its guidance into your daily life, you can enhance your well-being, gain clarity, and foster a deeper connection with the healing energies of crystals. Enjoy your journey and embrace the wisdom that each crystal offers.

Ayla,

When I think of you, I think of Rose Quartz, the stone of unconditional love.

This book is dedicated to you, a testament to the love and kindness you bring, and the joy you share with all.

With enduring love and appreciation,

The Answers You Seek

Are Within

Amethyst

Healing Energies

Known for its calming and purifying properties, Amethyst helps to clear the mind of negative thoughts and promotes emotional balance. It is also believed to enhance spiritual awareness and intuition.

Crystal Meditation

Sit in a quiet space with the Amethyst in your hand. Close your eyes and take deep breaths. Visualize a violet light surrounding the crystal and yourself. Repeat the mantra,

*"I am calm, I am purified,
I am connected to my higher self."*

Feel the Amethyst's energy merging with your own.

Rose Quartz

Healing Energies

The stone of unconditional love, Rose Quartz is believed to open the heart chakra, encouraging love, compassion, and forgiveness. It helps to heal emotional wounds and promotes self-love and inner peace.

Crystal Meditation

Hold the Rose Quartz close to your heart. Close your eyes and take slow, deep breaths. Imagine a soft pink light radiating from the crystal and enveloping your entire being. Chant the affirmation,

*"I am love, I am compassion,
I forgive and am forgiven."*

Feel the warmth and love filling your heart.

Citrine

Healing Energies

Known as the stone of abundance and manifestation, Citrine is believed to attract wealth, success, and prosperity. It also promotes positivity, creativity, and self-confidence.

Crystal Meditation

Place the Citrine in front of you and focus on it. Close your eyes and take a few deep breaths. Visualize a golden light emanating from the crystal, filling you with warmth and energy. Repeat the affirmation,

"I attract abundance, I am creative, I am confident."

Allow the energy to fill your entire being.

Clear Quartz

Healing Energies

Often called the "Master Healer," Clear Quartz is believed to amplify energy and thought, as well as the effects of other crystals. It enhances clarity, focus, and balance.

Crystal Meditation

Hold the Clear Quartz in your hands and close your eyes. Breathe deeply and visualize a bright white light surrounding the crystal and yourself. Repeat the mantra,

"I am clear, I am focused, I am balanced."

Feel the crystal's energy amplifying your intentions and thoughts.

Black Tourmaline

Healing Energies

Known for its protective properties, Black Tourmaline is believed to ward off negative energy and provide grounding. It also helps to reduce anxiety and stress, promoting a sense of calm and security.

Crystal Meditation

Sit comfortably with the Black Tourmaline in your hands. Close your eyes and take deep, grounding breaths. Visualize a shield of black light surrounding you, protecting you from negative energies. Chant the affirmation,

"I am protected, I am grounded, I am safe."

Feel the protective energy enveloping you.

Lapis Lazuli

Healing Energies

A stone of wisdom and truth, Lapis Lazuli is believed to enhance intellectual ability, stimulate the desire for knowledge, and improve communication. It also helps to reveal inner truths and promote self-awareness.

Crystal Meditation

Hold the Lapis Lazuli to your forehead (third eye) and close your eyes. Take deep breaths and visualize a deep blue light radiating from the crystal. Repeat the mantra,

"I am wise, I seek truth, I am aware."

Feel the energy enhancing your mind and communication.

Moonstone

Healing Energies

Associated with the divine feminine, Moonstone is believed to enhance intuition, emotional balance, and inner growth. It is also known to provide protection during travel, especially at night.

Crystal Meditation

Place the Moonstone on your palm and close your eyes. Take slow, deep breaths. Visualize a soft, glowing moonlight emanating from the crystal, filling you with serenity and intuition. Repeat the affirmation,

"I am intuitive, I am balanced, I grow with grace."

Feel the gentle energy soothing and guiding you.

Carnelian

Healing Energies

Known as the stone of motivation and endurance, Carnelian is believed to boost courage, confidence, and creativity. It helps to overcome procrastination and brings vitality and energy to the body.

Crystal Meditation

Hold the Carnelian in your hand and close your eyes. Breathe deeply and visualize a warm, orange light radiating from the crystal. Repeat the mantra, *"I am motivated, I am confident, I am creative."*
Feel the energy invigorating and empowering you.

Selenite

Healing Energies

Selenite is known for its cleansing and purifying properties. It is believed to clear negative energy, promote mental clarity, and enhance spiritual connection. It is also used for aura cleansing.

Crystal Meditation

Hold the Selenite above your head and close your eyes. Take deep breaths and visualize a pure, white light descending from the crystal and enveloping your body. Repeat the affirmation,

*"I am clear, I am pure,
I am connected."*

Feel the cleansing energy washing over you.

Aventurine

Healing Energies

Known as the stone of opportunity, Aventurine is believed to attract luck, abundance, and success. It also promotes emotional healing, calmness, and well-being.

Crystal Meditation

Hold the Aventurine in your hand and close your eyes. Breathe deeply and visualize a green light emanating from the crystal. Repeat the mantra,

"I am lucky, I am abundant, I am calm."

Feel the energy of opportunity and healing surrounding you.

Tiger's Eye

Healing Energies

Known for its grounding and protective properties, Tiger's Eye is believed to bring courage, strength, and personal power. It also helps to balance emotions and promote mental clarity.

Crystal Meditation

Hold the Tiger's Eye in your hand and close your eyes. Take deep breaths and visualize a golden-brown light radiating from the crystal. Repeat the affirmation,

"I am strong, I am courageous, I am balanced."

Feel the grounding and empowering energy filling you.

Hematite

Healing Energies

Hematite is known for its grounding and balancing properties. It is believed to absorb negative energy, reduce stress, and promote mental clarity and focus. It also enhances self-confidence and willpower.

Crystal Meditation

Hold the Hematite in your hand and close your eyes. Breathe deeply and visualize a dark, metallic light surrounding the crystal. Repeat the mantra,

"I am grounded, I am focused, I am confident."

Feel the grounding and balancing energy stabilizing you.

Amazonite

Healing Energies

Known as the stone of truth and courage, Amazonite is believed to enhance communication, dispel negative energy, and promote emotional balance. It also helps to soothe anxiety and calm the mind.

Crystal Meditation

Hold the Amazonite close to your throat and close your eyes. Take deep breaths and visualize a turquoise light radiating from the crystal. Repeat the affirmation,

"I speak my truth, I am courageous, I am balanced."

Feel the calming and empowering energy filling you.

Fluorite

Healing Energies

Known for its protective and stabilizing properties, Fluorite is believed to absorb and neutralize negative energy, enhance mental clarity, and promote focus. It also helps to balance emotions and improve decision-making.

Crystal Meditation

Hold the Fluorite in your hand and close your eyes. Breathe deeply and visualize a rainbow of light emanating from the crystal. Repeat the mantra,

"I am protected, I am focused, I am balanced."

Feel the stabilizing and clarifying energy enveloping you.

Labradorite

Healing Energies

Known as the stone of transformation and magic, Labradorite is believed to enhance intuition, protect against negative energy, and promote spiritual growth. It also helps to reveal hidden truths and awaken psychic abilities.

Crystal Meditation

Hold the Labradorite in your hand and close your eyes. Take deep breaths and visualize a shimmering, iridescent light surrounding the crystal. Repeat the affirmation,

"I am transformed, I am intuitive, I am protected."

Feel the magical and transformative energy filling you.

Pyrite

Healing Energies

Known as the stone of protection and abundance, Pyrite is believed to shield against negative energy, promote physical well-being, and attract wealth and success. It also enhances willpower and confidence.

Crystal Meditation

Hold the Pyrite in your hand and close your eyes. Breathe deeply and visualize a golden light emanating from the crystal. Repeat the mantra,

"I am protected, I am abundant, I am confident."

Feel the protective and empowering energy enveloping you.

Garnet

Healing Energies

Known for its energizing and revitalizing properties, Garnet is believed to boost vitality, passion, and creativity. It also promotes emotional balance and enhances relationships.

Crystal Meditation

Hold the Garnet in your hand and close your eyes. Take deep breaths and visualize a deep red light radiating from the crystal. Repeat the affirmation,

"I am energized, I am passionate, I am balanced."

Feel the revitalizing and balancing energy filling you.

Turquoise

Healing Energies

Known for its healing and protective properties, Turquoise is believed to enhance communication, promote emotional balance, and provide protection against negative energy. It also helps to soothe anxiety and stress.

Crystal Meditation

Hold the Turquoise in your hand and close your eyes. Breathe deeply and visualize a vibrant blue light surrounding the crystal. Repeat the mantra,

"I am healed, I am protected, I am calm."

Feel the soothing and protective energy enveloping you.

Malachite

Healing Energies

Known as the stone of transformation and protection, Malachite is believed to absorb negative energy, promote emotional healing, and enhance spiritual growth. It also helps to balance mood swings and reduce stress.

Crystal Meditation

Hold the Malachite in your hand and close your eyes. Take deep breaths and visualize a deep green light emanating from the crystal. Repeat the affirmation, *"I am transformed, I am healed, I am protected."*
Feel the transformative and protective energy filling you.

Smoky Quartz

Healing Energies

Known for its grounding and protective properties, Smoky Quartz is believed to absorb negative energy, promote emotional calmness, and enhance concentration. It also helps to alleviate stress and anxiety.

Crystal Meditation

Hold the Smoky Quartz in your hand and close your eyes. Breathe deeply and visualize a smoky light surrounding the crystal. Repeat the mantra,

"I am grounded, I am calm, I am protected."

Feel the grounding and calming energy stabilizing you.

Rhodonite

Healing Energies

Known for its emotional healing and balancing properties, Rhodonite is believed to promote love, compassion, and forgiveness. It helps to heal emotional wounds and encourages self-confidence and self-worth.

Crystal Meditation

Hold the Rhodonite in your hand and close your eyes. Take deep breaths and visualize a pink and black light radiating from the crystal. Repeat the affirmation,

"I am healed, I am loving, I am confident."

Feel the healing and balancing energy enveloping you.

Healing Energies

Known for its protective and healing properties, Jade is believed to attract good luck, abundance, and prosperity. It also promotes emotional balance, harmony, and well-being.

Crystal Meditation

Hold the Jade in your hand and close your eyes. Breathe deeply and visualize a green light surrounding the crystal. Repeat the mantra,

"I am lucky, I am abundant, I am balanced."

Feel the protective and healing energy filling you.

Obsidian

Healing Energies

Known for its protective and grounding properties, Obsidian is believed to shield against negative energy, promote emotional healing, and enhance clarity and truth. It also helps to release negative patterns and promote personal growth.

Crystal Meditation

Hold the Obsidian in your hand and close your eyes. Take deep breaths and visualize a black light emanating from the crystal. Repeat the affirmation,

"I am protected, I am clear, I am growing."

Feel the protective and grounding energy stabilizing you.

Blue Lace Agate

Healing Energies

Known for its calming and soothing properties, Blue Lace Agate is believed to promote communication, reduce anxiety, and enhance emotional healing. It also helps to calm the mind and promote tranquility.

Crystal Meditation

Hold the Blue Lace Agate close to your throat and close your eyes. Breathe deeply and visualize a soft blue light radiating from the crystal. Repeat the mantra,

"I am calm, I communicate with ease, I am at peace."

Feel the soothing and calming energy filling you.

Healing Energies

Known for its calming and soothing properties, Howlite is believed to reduce stress, anxiety, and anger. It also promotes patience, emotional healing, and a sense of inner peace.

Crystal Meditation

Hold the Howlite in your hand and close your eyes. Take deep breaths and visualize a white light with gray streaks surrounding the crystal. Repeat the affirmation,

"I am calm, I am patient, I am at peace."

Feel the calming and soothing energy enveloping you.

Chrysocolla

Healing Energies

Known for its calming and balancing properties, Chrysocolla is believed to promote communication, emotional healing, and inner strength. It also helps to reduce stress and anxiety.

Crystal Meditation

Hold the Chrysocolla in your hand and close your eyes. Breathe deeply and visualize a turquoise and green light radiating from the crystal. Repeat the mantra,

*"I am calm, I am strong,
I communicate with ease."*

Feel the calming and balancing energy filling you.

Lepidolite

Healing Energies

Known for its calming and stabilizing properties, Lepidolite is believed to reduce stress, anxiety, and depression. It also promotes emotional balance, tranquility, and a sense of well-being.

Crystal Meditation

Hold the Lepidolite in your hand and close your eyes. Take deep breaths and visualize a lavender light surrounding the crystal. Repeat the affirmation,

"I am calm, I am balanced, I am at peace."

Feel the calming and stabilizing energy enveloping you.

Angelite

Healing Energies

Known for its calming and soothing properties, Angelite is believed to promote spiritual awareness, communication with angels, and emotional healing. It also helps to reduce stress and anxiety.

Crystal Meditation

Hold the Angelite in your hand and close your eyes. Breathe deeply and visualize a soft blue light radiating from the crystal. Repeat the mantra,

"I am calm, I am connected, I am at peace."

Feel the soothing and calming energy filling you.

Bloodstone

Healing Energies

Known for its grounding and protective properties, Bloodstone is believed to enhance courage, strength, and vitality. It also promotes emotional balance, reduces stress, and enhances overall well-being.

Crystal Meditation

Hold the Bloodstone in your hand and close your eyes. Take deep breaths and visualize a deep green and red light surrounding the crystal. Repeat the affirmation,

"I am strong, I am courageous, I am balanced."

Feel the grounding and protective energy filling you.

Kyanite

Healing Energies

Known for its calming and balancing properties, Kyanite is believed to enhance communication, promote emotional healing, and protect against negative energy. It also helps to align the chakras and promote spiritual growth.

Crystal Meditation

Hold the Kyanite in your hand and close your eyes. Breathe deeply and visualize a blue light radiating from the crystal. Repeat the mantra,

"I am calm, I communicate with ease, I am aligned."

Feel the calming and balancing energy filling you.

Sunstone

Healing Energies

Known for its energizing and uplifting properties, Sunstone is believed to promote joy, positivity, and confidence. It also helps to reduce stress, increase vitality, and attract abundance.

Crystal Meditation

Hold the Sunstone in your hand and close your eyes. Take deep breaths and visualize a bright, golden light surrounding the crystal. Repeat the affirmation,

"I am joyful, I am positive, I am confident."

Feel the energizing and uplifting energy filling you.

Shungite

Healing Energies

Known for its protective and purifying properties, Shungite is believed to absorb negative energy, reduce stress, and promote physical and emotional well-being. It also helps to detoxify the body and improve overall health.

Crystal Meditation

Hold the Shungite in your hand and close your eyes. Breathe deeply and visualize a dark, protective light surrounding the crystal. Repeat the mantra,

"I am protected, I am purified, I am healthy."

Feel the protective and purifying energy enveloping you.

Apatite

Healing Energies

Known for its motivational and inspiring properties, Apatite is believed to enhance creativity, intellect, and personal growth. It also helps to reduce stress and promote emotional balance.

Crystal Meditation

Hold the Apatite in your hand and close your eyes. Take deep breaths and visualize a blue-green light radiating from the crystal. Repeat the affirmation,

"I am inspired, I am creative, I am balanced."

Feel the motivational and inspiring energy filling you.

Azurite

Healing Energies

Known for its spiritual and intellectual properties, Azurite is believed to enhance intuition, promote mental clarity, and stimulate creativity. It also helps to reduce stress and promote emotional healing.

Crystal Meditation

Hold the Azurite in your hand and close your eyes. Breathe deeply and visualize a deep blue light surrounding the crystal. Repeat the mantra,

"I am intuitive, I am clear, I am creative."

Feel the spiritual and intellectual energy filling you.

Moldavite

Healing Energies

Known for its transformative and spiritual properties, Moldavite is believed to enhance spiritual growth, promote emotional healing, and protect against negative energy. It also helps to awaken psychic abilities and promote personal growth.

Crystal Meditation

Hold the Moldavite in your hand and close your eyes. Take deep breaths and visualize a green light radiating from the crystal. Repeat the affirmation,

"I am transformed, I am healed, I am protected."

Feel the transformative and spiritual energy filling you.

Rhodochrosite

Healing Energies

Known for its emotional healing and balancing properties, Rhodochrosite is believed to promote love, compassion, and forgiveness. It also helps to heal emotional wounds and encourage self-love and self-worth.

Crystal Meditation

Hold the Rhodochrosite in your hand and close your eyes. Breathe deeply and visualize a pink and white light surrounding the crystal. Repeat the mantra,

"I am loved, I am compassionate, I am healed."

Feel the emotional healing and balancing energy filling you.

Onyx

Healing Energies

Known for its protective and grounding properties, Onyx is believed to absorb negative energy, promote emotional stability, and enhance self-control. It also helps to reduce stress and promote physical strength.

Crystal Meditation

Hold the Onyx in your hand and close your eyes. Take deep breaths and visualize a black light surrounding the crystal. Repeat the affirmation,

"I am protected, I am grounded, I am strong."

Feel the protective and grounding energy stabilizing you.

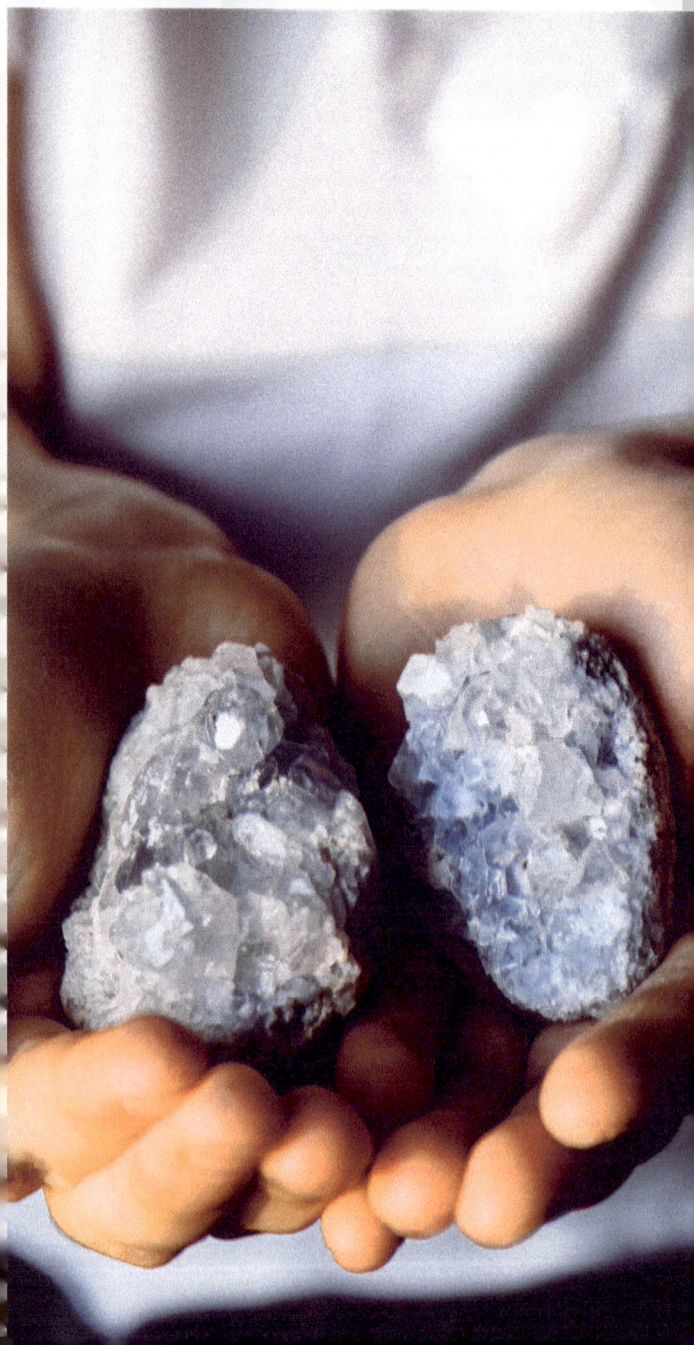

Celestite

Healing Energies

Known for its calming and soothing properties, Celestite is believed to promote spiritual awareness, communication with angels, and emotional healing. It also helps to reduce stress and anxiety.

Crystal Meditation

Hold the Celestite in your hand and close your eyes. Breathe deeply and visualize a soft blue light radiating from the crystal. Repeat the mantra,

"I am calm, I am connected, I am at peace."

Feel the soothing and calming energy filling you.

Garnierite

Healing Energies

Known for its transformative and heart-opening properties, Garnierite is believed to promote emotional healing, attract love and abundance, and enhance spiritual growth. It also helps to reduce stress and promote well-being.

Crystal Meditation

Hold the Garnierite in your hand and close your eyes. Take deep breaths and visualize a green and yellow light surrounding the crystal. Repeat the affirmation,

"I am transformed, I am loved, I am abundant."

Feel the transformative and heart-opening energy filling you.

Green Aventurine

Healing Energies

Known for its healing and balancing properties, Green Aventurine is believed to attract luck, abundance, and success. It also promotes emotional healing, calmness, and well-being.

Crystal Meditation

Hold the Green Aventurine in your hand and close your eyes. Breathe deeply and visualize a green light surrounding the crystal. Repeat the mantra,

"I am lucky, I am abundant, I am healed."

Feel the healing and balancing energy filling you.

Red Jasper

Healing Energies

Known for its grounding and nurturing properties, Jasper is believed to provide stability, protection, and emotional balance. It also helps to reduce stress, enhance relaxation, and promote overall well-being.

Crystal Meditation

Hold the Jasper in your hand and close your eyes. Take deep breaths and visualize a warm, earthy light surrounding the crystal. Repeat the affirmation,

"I am grounded, I am protected, I am balanced."

Feel the grounding and nurturing energy stabilizing you.

Aquamarine

Healing Energies

Known for its calming and soothing properties, Aquamarine is believed to promote communication, reduce stress, and enhance emotional healing. It also helps to calm the mind and promote tranquility.

Crystal Meditation

Hold the Aquamarine in your hand and close your eyes. Breathe deeply and visualize a soft blue-green light radiating from the crystal. Repeat the mantra,
"I am calm, I communicate with ease, I am at peace."
Feel the calming and soothing energy filling you.

Emerald

Healing Energies

Known for its healing and heart-opening properties, Emerald is believed to promote love, compassion, and forgiveness. It also helps to heal emotional wounds, attract abundance, and enhance spiritual growth.

Crystal Meditation

Hold the Emerald in your hand and close your eyes. Take deep breaths and visualize a vibrant green light surrounding the crystal. Repeat the affirmation,

"I am loved, I am compassionate, I am healed."

Feel the healing and heart-opening energy filling you.

Kunzite

Healing Energies

Known for its heart-opening and calming properties, Kunzite is believed to promote love, compassion, and emotional healing. It also helps to reduce stress, calm the mind, and enhance spiritual awareness.

Crystal Meditation

Hold the Kunzite in your hand and close your eyes. Breathe deeply and visualize a soft pink and lavender light radiating from the crystal. Repeat the mantra,

"I am loved, I am calm, I am healed."

Feel the heart-opening and calming energy filling you.

Peridot

Healing Energies

Known for its cleansing and healing properties, Peridot is believed to promote emotional balance, reduce stress, and enhance overall well-being. It also helps to attract abundance and protect against negative energy.

Crystal Meditation

Hold the Peridot in your hand and close your eyes. Take deep breaths and visualize a bright green light surrounding the crystal. Repeat the affirmation,

"I am cleansed, I am balanced, I am abundant."

Feel the cleansing and healing energy filling you.

Healing Energies

Known for its energizing and inspiring properties, Topaz is believed to enhance creativity, promote emotional balance, and attract abundance. It also helps to reduce stress, increase vitality, and promote overall well-being.

Crystal Meditation

Hold the Topaz in your hand and close your eyes. Breathe deeply and visualize a golden light radiating from the crystal. Repeat the mantra,

"I am inspired, I am creative, I am abundant."

Feel the energizing and inspiring energy filling you.

Unakite

Healing Energies

Known for its healing and balancing properties, Unakite is believed to promote emotional healing, reduce stress, and enhance overall well-being. It also helps to attract love and abundance.

Crystal Meditation

Hold the Unakite in your hand and close your eyes. Take deep breaths and visualize a green and pink light surrounding the crystal. Repeat the affirmation,

"I am healed, I am balanced, I am abundant."

Feel the healing and balancing energy filling you.

Sapphire

Healing Energies

Sapphire is known as the stone of wisdom and royalty. It is believed to enhance mental clarity, focus, and self-discipline, making it a powerful ally for those seeking to achieve their goals. Sapphire is also associated with protection, bringing spiritual insight and helping to calm the mind.

Crystal Meditation

Sit comfortably with the Sapphire in your hand or placed on your third eye chakra. Close your eyes and take deep, calming breaths. Visualize a deep blue light radiating from the Sapphire, Repeat the affirmation,

"I am clear, focused, and wise."
Feel Sapphire's energy enhance your mental clarity and spiritual insight.

Larimar

Healing Energies

Known for its calming and soothing properties, Larimar is believed to promote emotional healing, reduce stress, and enhance communication. It also helps to calm the mind and promote tranquility.

Crystal Meditation

Hold the Larimar in your hand and close your eyes. Take deep breaths and visualize a soft blue light radiating from the crystal. Repeat the mantra,
"I am calm, I communicate with ease, I am at peace."
Feel the calming and soothing energy filling you.

Tanzanite

Healing Energies

Known for its transformative and spiritual properties, Tanzanite is believed to enhance spiritual growth, promote emotional healing, and protect against negative energy. It also helps to awaken psychic abilities and promote personal growth.

Crystal Meditation

Hold the Tanzanite in your hand and close your eyes. Breathe deeply and visualize a violet and blue light surrounding the crystal. Repeat the mantra,

"I am transformed, I am healed, I am protected."

Feel the transformative and spiritual energy filling you.

Ametrine

Healing Energies

Known for its balancing and healing properties, Ametrine is believed to promote emotional balance, reduce stress, and enhance overall well-being. It also helps to attract abundance and promote personal growth.

Crystal Meditation

Hold the Ametrine in your hand and close your eyes. Take deep breaths and visualize a purple and yellow light surrounding the crystal. Repeat the affirmation,

"I am balanced, I am healed, I am abundant."

Feel the balancing and healing energy filling you.

Morganite

Healing Energies

Known for its heart-opening and calming properties, Morganite is believed to promote love, compassion, and emotional healing. It also helps to reduce stress, calm the mind, and enhance spiritual awareness.

Crystal Meditation

Hold the Morganite in your hand and close your eyes. Breathe deeply and visualize a soft pink light radiating from the crystal. Repeat the mantra,

*"I am loved, I am calm,
I am healed."*

Feel the heart-opening and calming energy filling you.

Sodalite

Healing Energies

Known for its calming and balancing properties, Sodalite is believed to enhance communication, promote emotional healing, and protect against negative energy. It also helps to align the chakras and promote spiritual growth.

Crystal Meditation

Hold the Sodalite in your hand and close your eyes. Take deep breaths and visualize a blue and white light surrounding the crystal. Repeat the affirmation,

"I am calm, I communicate with ease, I am balanced."

Feel the calming and balancing energy filling you.

Sugilite

Healing Energies

Known for its spiritual and healing properties, Sugilite is believed to promote spiritual growth, enhance intuition, and protect against negative energy. It also helps to reduce stress and promote emotional healing.

Crystal Meditation

Hold the Sugilite in your hand and close your eyes. Breathe deeply and visualize a purple light radiating from the crystal. Repeat the mantra,

"I am intuitive, I am protected, I am healed."

Feel the spiritual and healing energy filling you.

Prehnite

Healing Energies

Known for its healing and protective properties, Prehnite is believed to promote emotional balance, reduce stress, and enhance overall well-being. It also helps to attract abundance and protect against negative energy.

Crystal Meditation

Hold the Prehnite in your hand and close your eyes. Take deep breaths and visualize a green and white light surrounding the crystal. Repeat the affirmation,

"I am healed, I am balanced, I am protected."

Feel the healing and protective energy filling you.

Crystal Reflections

Crystal Reflections...

Crystal Reflections...

Crystal Reflections...

Crystal Reflections...

Crystal Reflections...

Crystal Reflections...

Crystal Reflections...

Crystal Reflections...

Crystal Reflections...

Crystal Reflections...

Crystal Reflections...

Crystal Reflections...

Crystal Reflections...

Crystal Reflections...

Crystal Reflections...

Crystal Reflections...

Crystal Reflections...

Crystal Reflections...

Crystal Reflections...

Crystal Reflections...

Crystal Reflections...

Crystal Reflections...

Crystal Reflections...

Crystal Reflections...

Crystal Reflections...

Crystal Reflections...

Crystal Reflections...

Crystal Reflections...

Crystal Reflections...

Crystal Reflections...

Crystal Reflections...

Crystal Reflections...

Crystal Reflections...

Crystal Reflections...

Crystal Reflections...

Crystal Reflections...

Crystal Reflections...

Crystal Reflections...

Crystal Reflections...

Crystal Reflections...

Crystal Reflections...

Crystal Reflections...

Crystal Reflections...

Crystal Reflections...

Crystal Reflections...

Crystal Reflections...

Crystal Reflections...

Crystal Reflections...

Crystal Reflections...

Crystal Reflections...

Crystal Reflections...

The "Daily Guidance" series offers an innovative approach to finding spiritual wisdom and practical advice. Each book in the series is a unique tool designed for daily introspection and decision-making. Readers are invited to meditate on a question or seek general guidance for the day, then flip to a random page in the book. The page they land on provides a personalized message from various spiritual sources, such as angels, tarot, or spirit animals. With each turn of the page, these books deliver insightful, positive messages and mantras to inspire personal growth and provide clarity on life's daily challenges and decisions.

Other books in this series:-
The Angelic Oracles
Daily Angel Tarot Reading
Mystic Tarot Cat
Oracle of the Tarot Cat
Vibes Unveiled
Spirit Animal Oracle
Answers from the Oracles
Messages from the Angels

More on the Bookshelves at
www.korupublishing.com

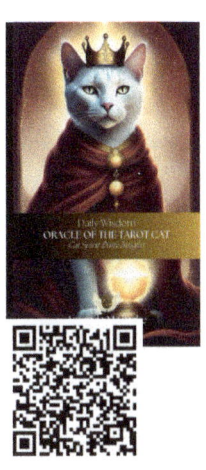

More on the Bookshelves at www.korupublishing.com

www.ingramcontent.com/pod-product-compliance
Lightning Source LLC
Chambersburg PA
CBHW061736070526
44585CB00024B/2693